The Truth About Cats

The Truth About CATS

BERNICE THOMAS
with photographs by Beuford Smith

Thomas Congdon Books
E. P. DUTTON · New York

Copyright © 1979 by Bernice Thomas
Photographs copyright © 1979
by Beuford Smith/Césaire Photo Agency
All rights reserved. Printed in the U.S.A.

No part of this publication may be reproduced
or transmitted in any form or by any means, electronic
or mechanical, including photocopying, recording or any information
storage and retrieval system now known or to be invented, without permission
in writing from the publisher, except by a reviewer who wishes to quote brief passages
in connection with a review written for inclusion in a magazine, newspaper or broadcast.

For information contact: E. P. Dutton, 2 Park Avenue, New York N.Y. 10016

Library of Congress Cataloging in Publication Data
Thomas, Bernice.   The truth about cats.
1. Cats—Training.   2. Cats.   "Thomas Congdon Books."   I. Title.
SF446.6.T47   1979   636.8'08'3   79-12764
ISBN: 0-525-04475-2

Published simultaneously in Canada by Clarke, Irwin & Company Limited,
Toronto and Vancouver

10 9 8 7 6 5 4 3 2 1
First Edition

For every kind of beast and bird, of reptile and sea creature, can be tamed and has been tamed by humankind.
—JAMES 3:7

Contents

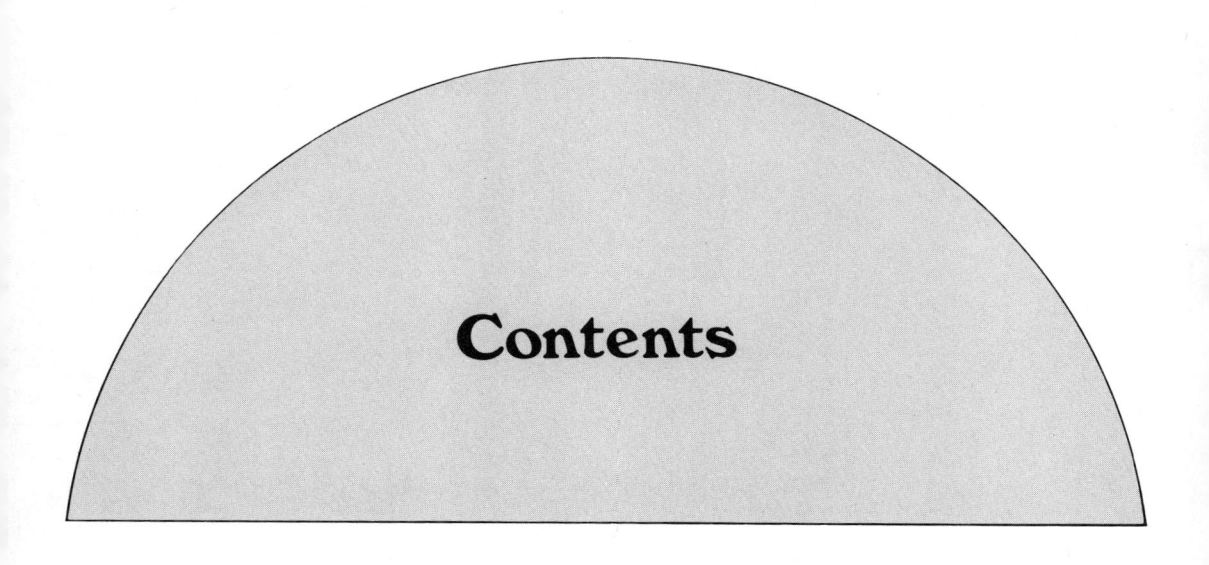

Introduction ix

1
The Truth About Cats 1

2
Preparation for Training 5

3
Training 15

4
Etiquette 43

5
Grooming and Exercise 48

6
Diet 57

7
General Care 62

Conclusion 67

Introduction

The purpose of this book is to explode once and for all the myths associated with cats. It is intended for those who suspect that there is room for improvement where cats are concerned. It is also intended for cat-haters who believe that cats are worthless creatures.

Some people might ask, why train a cat? Or why train a cat to act like a dog? Well, my answer is why not? Would anyone ask these foolish questions of a dog trainer or a horse trainer? Certainly not. So why should cats be excluded from obedience training?

There are many people who do not like dogs for various reasons but like the fact that they can be taught many useful things. There are also those people who can't keep dogs because their landlord disapproves. For these people, a properly trained cat could be an ideal pet and a worthwhile companion.

This book is intended only for those who are ready to hear the truth about cats.

The Truth About Cats

1

The Truth About Cats

The truth about cats is that they are not aloof, lazy, disrespectful, or impossible to teach. In fact, they are quite trainable—as trainable as dogs or circus animals. Lions and tigers are, after all, just big cats.

Obedience-trained cats respect and obey their owners. They learn to perform—jumping over hurdles, through hoops, and from platform to platform. They are happy, healthy, affectionate, and eager to please. And they have a good time. In this book I will show you how to train your cat, not only to do tricks, but also to eat a healthy diet and to get proper exercise.

The common mythology about cats is that they are either too stupid or too "independent" to be trained. People have refused to accept the fact that cats have brains and can think intelligently. Over the centuries, they have either worshipped cats or used them to kill rodents. Had people begun training them thousands of years ago, there would now be a recognized training method for cats. Cat shows, which now have only beauty classes, would have obedience classes as well. Wouldn't it be nice to watch a group of highly trained, well-mannered cats performing tricks and competing against each other, instead of looking at a bunch of pampered, spoiled do-nothings?

Many people still make the mistake of either talking down to their cats or looking up to them. Those who talk down to cats do so because "everyone knows" cats will not learn. These people underestimate the cat's ability. The cat senses he's not expected to learn, so he doesn't try.

The owner who looks up to his cat, on the other hand, actually thinks that the ugly habits of cats, such as hissing, growling, scratching, and refusing to learn, are "charming." According to him, these characteristics are evidence of the cat's "independence" and "intelligence." It is interesting to note that a person would hate such traits in a human friend. A mother cat would severely discipline her kittens if they behaved this way. But this owner gives in to his cat's every demand. He seems to enjoy being dominated by his pet. The cat soon senses that he is the boss, loses respect for his owner, and refuses to learn.

The person who hates cats and doesn't want to own them at all thinks cats are self-absorbed, rude, disobedient, and are only interested in their owners when they want something, usually food. Such a cat is certainly a spoiled brat, but your cat need not be one.

•

When I was a child, my parents gave me many different animals as pets. The animal I liked best was the cat. I had many kittens and cats, but no one in my family ever tried to teach them anything—we all "knew" they wouldn't learn. I could never even teach them basic things, such as learning to use the litter pan regularly, or not to scratch the furniture. So they grew up to resent any discipline. I gave away quite a few cats because they developed unpleasant dispositions. Still, I saw something good in cats. They had confidence, strength, and determination. I continued to look for a cat that possessed these qualities but would also maintain a loving temperament.

As I grew older, I began to wonder if it was possible to train cats. Was their so-called independence fact or myth? If a cat were trained, would it then be more willing to please its owner and to abandon its disagreeable habits? Although cats are stubborn and reserved, while dogs are outgoing and anxious to please, I had always thought cats were intelligent animals. Maybe they could even learn to do tricks like dogs. I decided to prove that they could!

My first test kitten was Sam, a three-month-old Siamese chocolate point, bought from a local pet shop. I began training him at five months, first teaching him to walk on a leash. It took him two weeks to learn. Then I began teaching him to come when called. He was learning very quickly, when he suddenly came down with pneumonia and died.

After Sam's death I lost interest in my project. It was three years later when I tried again. This time I found my kitten, Jason, at the ASPCA. I wanted to see if an ordinary mixed-breed domestic shorthair could learn as fast as my purebred Siamese. Jason was a dark gray, six-week-old kitten. He was very sick when I got him. Six weeks later his condition was still very bad. A doctor gave me medicine for him and told me to feed him baby food, but said I should have him put to sleep if there was no improvement within a few days. By that time I had become attached to this sickly little animal and didn't want to lose him. Happily, he responded to the medicine and was cured.

Once he had recovered, I decided to set an example with him. He would not eat my plants or scratch my furniture; he would be clean and well trained. He would be, in other words, the perfect house cat. And indeed, he was.

My next kitten was Kelly, the white cat shown in several pictures in this book. Kelly is also an average domestic cat. I began to train him at the age of six weeks, to see if such a young kitten would be able to learn. I also wanted to prove to myself that my cats were not flukes—that any ordinary cat could be trained. And Kelly too, as you can see, has learned to do tricks. He is also a lovely, well-mannered cat.

I trained another eleven kittens and cats before writing this book. Some were fast learners; some were slow. But they all learned. I am convinced that any cat can learn what I've set forth here.

•

The training program requires you to be smarter than your cat at all times. A cat is stronger willed than many animals and to teach it you must display great confidence and determination. Do not let setbacks upset or discourage you. Tell yourself, "My cat will learn."

Think positively. When the cat realizes you won't give in to him, he will not only settle down to learn, he will actually *want* to please you.

Do not be afraid that if you train your cat he will lose his individuality and become a robotlike creature. Can you honestly imagine a cat losing his personality? The only personality differences between trained and untrained cats are that obedience-trained cats appear to be smarter and are less obstinate. They are not bored, spoiled brats. Instead, they are well-adjusted, even-tempered animals who are attentive to their owners and who enjoy pleasing them. Doing tricks gives them a sense of pride and accomplishment and keeps them busy and in good shape. These cats are fun to play with, and they have fun themselves.

For this book I selected a new kitten, Aaron. He is the little tiger-stripe you see in the pictures. I started training him when he was just two months old. Within two weeks, he had mastered everything. Your cat may take longer, but he will learn.

At the ASPCA, the author selects a kitten to train for this book.

Preparation for Training

This chapter covers the things you need to do and know before you start a training program for your cat.

Selecting the Right Kitten

When you are looking for a kitten to train, don't just buy the first cute kitten you see. Make sure you choose one you find particularly appealing, one with whom you have a good rapport. I saw at least forty kittens before I found Jason, but the moment I saw him I knew he was the right one. It will make training much easier if you have a kitten you think is very special.

I also feel that it's best to establish a one-to-one relationship with your new kitten. Once the cat realizes you are the one person he can depend on, he will pay special attention to you and will be easier to train. The kitten who has a number of people feeding and caring for him will learn that if one person doesn't give him what he wants, another will. He will become fussy and demanding. The cat who has one master will be more obedient, and more affectionate as well.

The Best Age for Training

It is always best to start training a cat at a young age. In fact, the younger the better. A six-week-old kitten is not too young to learn and will actually be easy to teach because he is curious and receptive.

A young kitten will understand what you expect of him, but you may have some trouble keeping his attention. A kitten five weeks to four months old cannot be expected to remember fully all the tricks he learned the previous day. It is therefore important to repeat each trick every day during a fifteen-minute session. When the cat gets to be four or five months old, you can eliminate these practice lessons.

Aaron is eight weeks old at the start—a bright, alert pupil.

Words and Hand Signals

One of the problems with training cats, I believe, is that many of them do not seem to understand human words. They will try to sense what you're saying, but they usually respond much better to visual commands than to spoken ones.

I have trained most of my cats to hand signals and finger-snapping. As an experiment, I have then tried to change over to word commands. This method was a shock to the cats—they would hiss, swish their tails, flatten their ears against their heads, and act generally bewildered. They seemed to be unsure of whether or not they were doing the right thing. When I went back to hand signals and finger-snapping, the cats rushed to do their tricks as usual.

Cats are best directed by hand signals. This one means "stop."

Cats, like dogs, can be made to come—at a snap of the fingers.

A cat's confused behavior when faced with word commands could quite easily be misunderstood as a display of independence, refusal to learn, or stupidity. In my experience, however, it usually indicates that the cat just doesn't understand what you're telling him. Of course, such behavior may be an act of defiance. If it is (and only you can interpret your own cat's actions), it probably means the cat has been spoiled and has no respect for your orders. In that case, it will take persistence and a lot of work to train him to obey you.

All commands should be short and uncomplicated. A cat that does respond to words will do better if you use one word rather than two or three. Say "paw," instead of "give me your paw."

Hand signals should also be simple. For example, when you want your cat to stop, raise the flat of your hand in front of his face and say "stop," loud enough to get his attention. Soon the cat will recognize the signal without the word. Finger-snapping is also very useful. Start by using this signal to get your cat to come to you. Say "come" and snap your fingers. Within two days the cat will respond to the finger-snapping alone. I also use this signal to get the cats to start their tricks.

8 *The Truth About Cats*

Leash and Collar

A kitten can be taught to wear a collar and leash at six weeks of age. You will need to leash train your kitten in order to teach him tricks. You can also walk him on a leash, indoors or out, which is good exercise (see Chapter Five). My cats do not wear their collars all the time—only for walks and training.

A collar for a very young kitten should be lightweight and washable. When the kitten gets older, you can get him a collar made of good-quality leather or chain. I use a chain leash, which lasts longer than leather or plastic. The leash should have fairly large links because all cats pull some while walking on a leash, even well-trained cats that heel. It's best to buy a well-made leash early.

For training, I often use heavy string instead of a leash. Just make a loop in the end to serve as a collar. This type of leash is especially good for guiding a cat through his tricks because it is small and doesn't interfere with what he's doing. You can see Aaron wearing such a leash in some of the pictures.

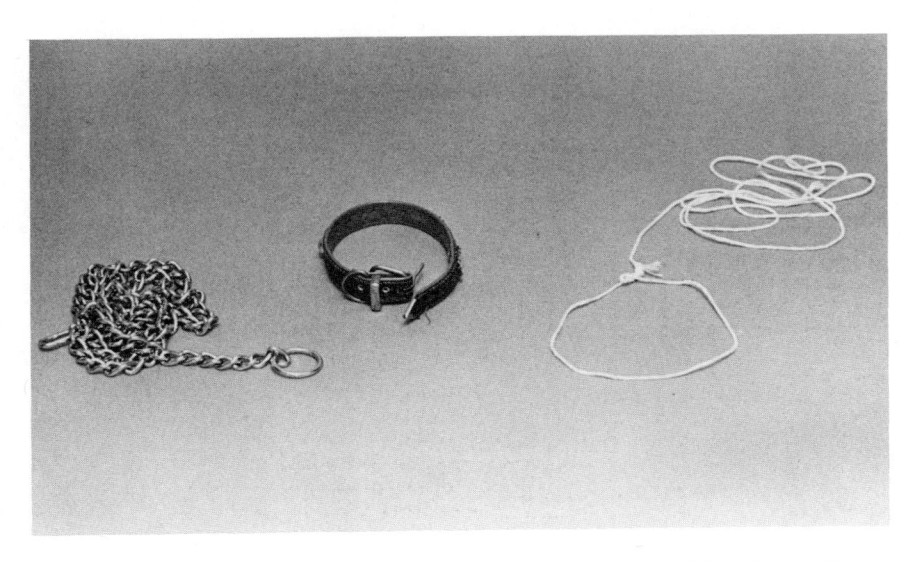

These are essential for a cat training program—a good leather collar, a chain leash for walking the cat out of doors, and a heavy string training leash.

The Location of Training Sessions

It is important to vary the location of training sessions right from the beginning. Do not practice in the same place day after day. If you do, the cat will become so accustomed to performing in one place that he will refuse to perform anywhere else. The cat will act like a robot. He will know all his tricks backward and forward and will rush to perform them, but if you take him to a new location, he will be completely lost and confused.

Changing the location of his tricks forces him to think and develops his confidence.

Scolding and Praise

You will have to scold your cat occasionally in the course of training. Whenever he disobeys, growls, or hisses, yell at him in a loud voice. He will understand from your tone that you are displeased.

An accusing finger lets Aaron know the author is angry.

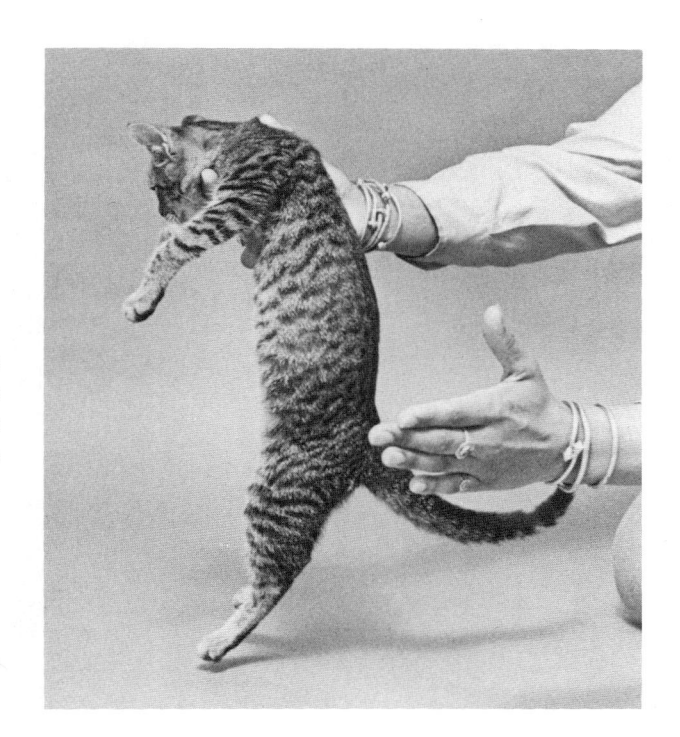

Aaron gets a light swat on the bottom when he's really uncooperative. He's unhurt, but he takes notice.

If he still refuses to do things your way, slap him slightly on the hindquarters. This will not hurt him. Be firm. Do not let him get the upper hand. Remember that you are the boss. Always be sure to scold him immediately when he does something wrong, because if you delay, he may no longer understand why you're angry.

Some cats resent being scolded and react by brooding. Such a cat may hide away in a secluded spot, avoid you during the day, or simply have a "hurt" look on his face. He is trying to make you feel ashamed of having treated him badly. If he wants to brood, let him. When he realizes you are not going to worry about him, he will drop this attitude. You may want to reassure him with love and petting, but don't overdo it. Remember that you have scolded him for a *very good reason*. Let him know that he is forgiven, but that his behavior is not condoned.

The other side of scolding is praise. Be sure to praise your cat whenever he does what you ask. Pet him, hold him, and talk softly

Preparation for Training

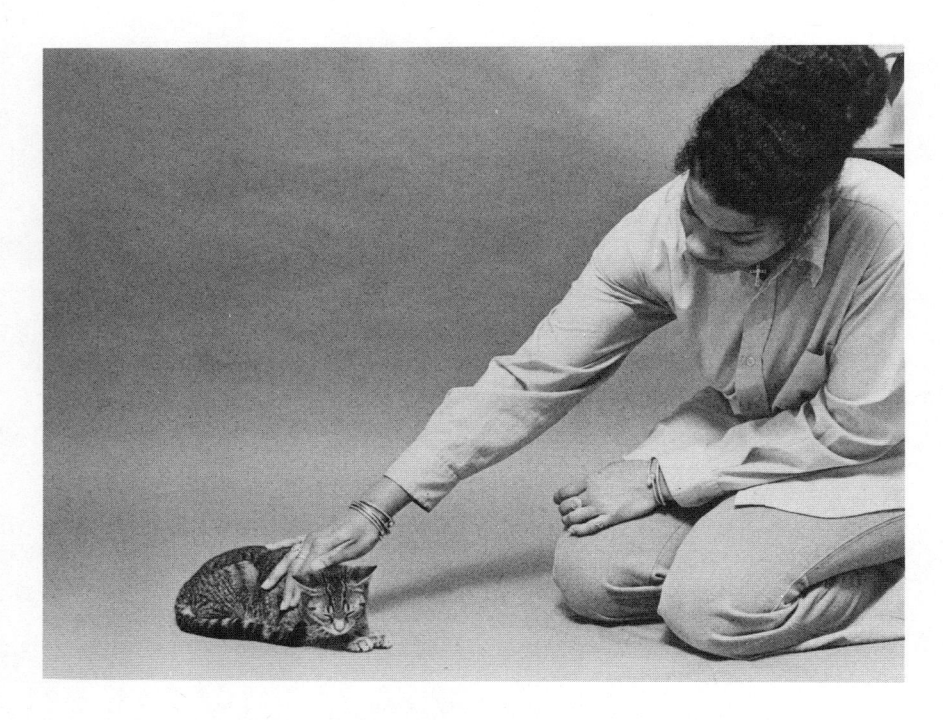

Of course, when he succeeds, he's praised and petted.

to him. Do not withdraw affection, even when he is stubborn and difficult. Let him know when you are angry, but always be sure he knows you like him.

Rewards

I am strongly opposed to giving food rewards to a cat for doing his tricks properly. The average house cat gets three meals a day, a place to sleep, and lots of love. He doesn't need a treat. His rewards should be praise, affection, and petting.

When your cat is given a reward to make him perform, he is not doing the trick because he wants to obey you. He is merely doing it to get the treat. Such an animal will almost never perform on a full stomach, and he will stop performing entirely when he tires of the treat. Do you want a cat who has to be bribed to please you?

Work—Not Play

It is important to establish at the first lesson that trick learning is work, not play. A young kitten will want to play with you whenever you try to start teaching him. If you let him think of this as playtime, he will ignore your commands and refuse to take his lessons seriously.

To discourage playing, yell "no" and lightly slap the kitten's hindquarters. He should calm down immediately. You must be careful, however, not to let him think you are punishing him. If you are too strict, he may resent his lessons or become afraid. *Never let this happen.* Be firm—but *loving.* Doing tricks should be fun for your cat.

Playing with the string leash makes it seem familiar and friendly.

Preparation for Training 13

Once the kitten gets used to the training sessions, you will notice that he becomes more serious at that time and reverts to his playful self afterward. This shows you have made tremendous progress.

Some very young kittens will naturally be afraid during the first few training sessions. Kelly, my white cat, even tried to run away. Reassure a frightened cat with lots of praise and affection. After a while, he will lose his fear. Kelly did, and began learning everything in record time.

The Correct Attitude Is Essential

You, as the master, must have a strong positive attitude about your cat. You are the boss. If you convey this to your pet, he will respond. Some cats are naturally docile; others are difficult. But they can all be disciplined. Cats are headstrong and bad-tempered only because their owners allow them to be. If a cat sees he can get everything he wants without having to do anything for it, he will naturally continue his disobedient ways. It's up to you to show him who is in control.

For example, when I first got Sam, he was a terrible disciplinary problem. I couldn't even train him to use his litter pan. One day when he used my new rug, I grabbed him and said, "Sam, you will never do this again!" I talked to him as though he were a person. I told him in no uncertain terms that if he didn't shape up he would be thrown out of my house. I returned him several times to the "scene of the crime" and told him that he should be ashamed of himself. I believed he could understand me—and so he did. After that day he always used his pan and never made another mistake.

As I've said before, you must always be smarter than your cat. Do not let him dominate you. Be firm. Make him respect you. But be gentle and affectionate as well. Let your cat know you love him. He will want to return your affection by behaving himself and doing things that please you.

3
Training

I have trained fifteen cats and kittens to do the tricks described in this book and have found the job easy every time. Some cats learned faster than others, but they *all* learned. The training process requires you to be patient and firm. Let your cat know that this is serious business and that you expect a lot from him. Do not allow him to get away with temper tantrums or laziness. Be sure he knows you are the boss. You will soon have a beautifully trained cat who wants to please you. Do not be afraid your cat will lose his individuality or strength of character. He will not. He will lose only his spoiled brat qualities. And you and he will have a new game to play together.

Leash Training

The first thing to teach your cat is how to walk on a leash. Once he submits to a leash, he loses his "I am the king" attitude and allows himself to trust you and learn from you. It will then be easy to teach him to do tricks, using the leash as an important training aid.

There is no special trick to leash training. Just put the collar and leash, or long string, on your cat. If he's very uncomfortable, have him wear the collar for a couple of days to get used to it. Then attach the leash and walk with him from room to room. He will pull away and fight a lot at first, but be firm. Push him from behind when he refuses to follow you. Make sure you don't hurt him by pulling on the leash, but give it a gentle tug to let him know you want him to come. Work with him for half an hour every day. You will find that at some point he will suddenly give in and decide to go along with you. With my cats Sam and Jason, this happened during the second week. Kelly and Aaron, however, took only a few days. After the cat accepts the leash, it will be another few days before he walks perfectly at all times.

At this point you can teach your cat to walk on the leash outdoors. It's good exercise, and cats like to get some fresh air. It's best at first

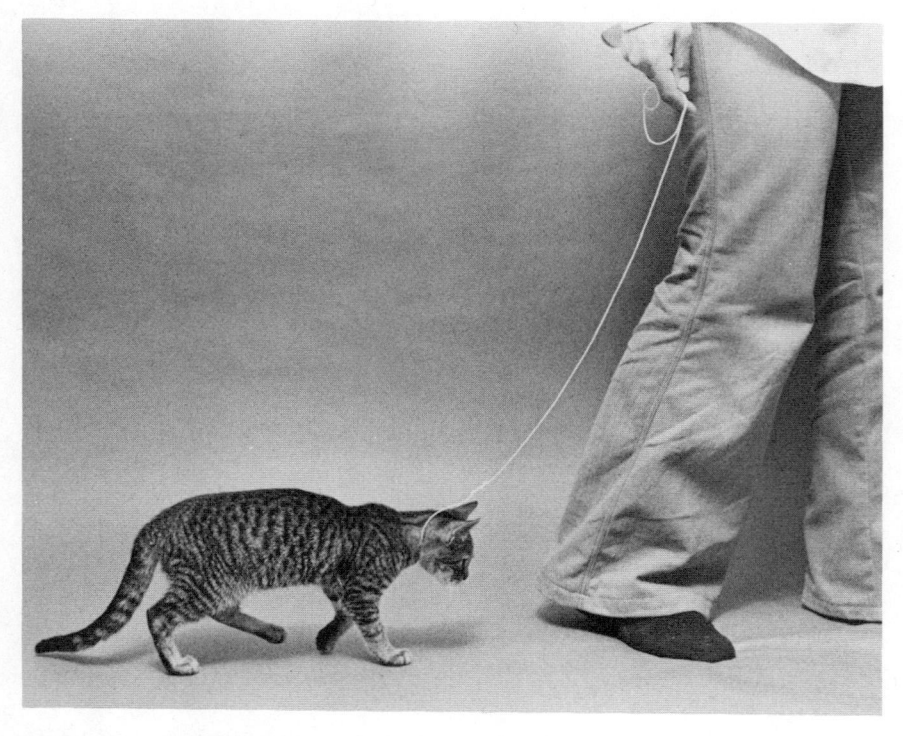

Aaron's first accomplishment—walking on a leash.

16 *The Truth About Cats*

to take the cat outside at a time when there are few people about and very little danger of running into dogs. Some cats are more nervous than others about being outdoors. You might try taking a kitten to the park and letting him play in the grass for a few days before you try to walk him. An older cat can sit in your lap watching the scenery until he gets used to being outside. In general, the younger a cat is when you start taking him out, the less frightened he will be. Take the cat out for about thirty minutes every day. If he is scared, reassure him with petting and lots of attention. When I first took Jason out, he was terrified—meowing and shivering. Within four days, however, he was walking outdoors with the high-stepping gait of a greyhound, head held high. He looked great.

Heeling

You should teach your cat to heel once he's used to the leash. Whenever he crosses in front or in back of you, say "no" and return him to the proper side. You may have to slap him lightly. Be persistent. Your cat should learn to heel within two to four days. Use the same training method if the cat keeps walking when you stop. Soon he will walk without pulling or hanging back.

When I began to train Sam he fought so much that I began to think cat training *was* impossible. I got so discouraged I was about to give up when all of a sudden Sam gave in and walked fine. This happened during the second week of training. Jason also took that long to learn, but Kelly and Aaron took only a few days.

Teaching the Cat to Come When Called

The next step is to teach your cat to come when called. This is the most important trick he will learn, and it is the basis of all the other tricks. Again, you need patience and persistence. Learning may take a few weeks, a few days, or, as with Kelly, less than an hour. Once your cat comes to you on command, the rest of the training is simple.

Put the leash on your cat and place the cat three feet in front of you in a sitting position. Then gently pull him toward you with the leash while saying "come" and snapping your fingers. Repeat this twenty or thirty times a day. Continue the lesson until the cat comes to you immediately, without hesitation, even before you pull on the leash. He will probably learn to respond best to the finger-snapping.

Now begin to place the cat farther away from you, using a long string as a leash. Continue this lesson until you can call him from a distance of twenty feet.

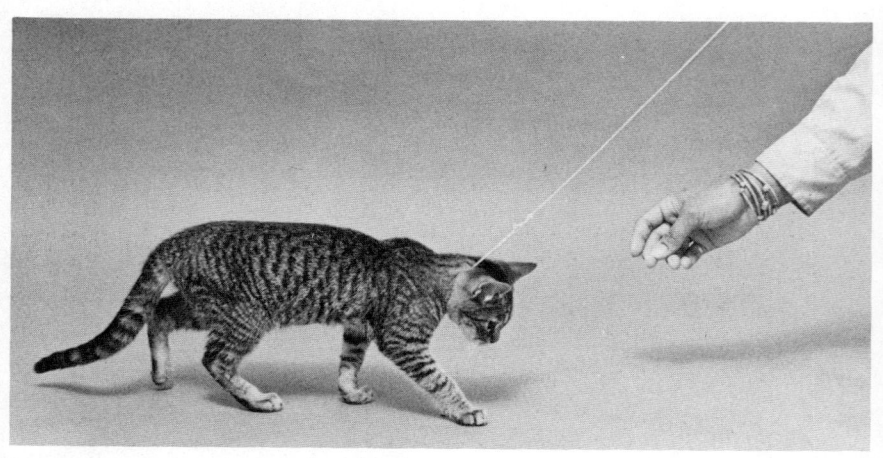

A couple of tugs on the leash at first, and after a few lessons Aaron comes on command.

18 *The Truth About Cats*

At this point, you can begin to train him to come without the leash. This will be more difficult because the cat assumes that when he's off the leash, his training has stopped. It's up to you to persuade him otherwise.

Again set the cat three feet in front of you, with the leash on, and have him come to you. Then remove the leash and do the same. If he looks puzzled and doesn't come, gently put your hand on his hindquarters and push him forward toward you, while saying "come." When he reaches you, be sure to pet and praise him. Repeat this twenty or thirty times, until he has the idea that training doesn't stop when the leash is off. If he's learned to come properly with the leash on, it should not take more than a few days to teach him to come without the leash. If he shows no signs of learning, scold him when he doesn't come. He's just trying to ignore you and get the upper hand. Once he realizes you're serious, you'll be amazed at how fast he can learn.

Affection is the reward for a lesson well-learned.

Stopping

When your cat comes on command without the leash, from a distance of fifteen to thirty feet, you can consider him trained. Now you should teach him to stop on command. Call your cat. While he is walking toward you, raise your hand and say "stop," while reaching out to stop him. Repeat this lesson twenty or thirty times a day, until the cat stops as soon as he sees your hand go up. Then say "come" again, or snap your fingers, and he will resume walking. It may take time for the cat to learn all this, but do not lose faith. He will learn, *if* you are forceful and stubborn.

Jumping Onto a Stand

The next step is to teach your cat to jump onto a low stand. I use a plastic Parson's table, available from any department store. With a young kitten you might want to start with a big, thick book—the phone book, if you live in a large city.

Place the cat four feet in front of you and have him come. Praise him for this. Now put him four feet in front of you, but this time place the stand in his path. Order him to come. When he reaches the stand, his first thought will be to go around it to get to you. Hold up your hand while saying "stop" or "no." Then place him in front of the stand and push him onto it while saying "come." Repeat this lesson several times a day until the cat goes onto the stand without your help.

Leash on, Aaron learns his first real trick. He has to be nudged once or twice, but he makes it . . . up, over, and down.

Training 21

You may find it helpful to use the leash for this training. Put the leash on the cat and gently pull the cat toward you while saying "come." The cat may be more willing to go onto the stand when his leash is on. Once he is doing this trick to your command, before you pull on the leash, you can take the leash off and repeat the procedure. Continue until he has mastered the trick.

This lesson may take as long as two or three days to teach, if you spend fifteen minutes to a half hour each day on the training. As the cat becomes more experienced, slowly raise the height of the stand. Even a kitten can jump up to a two-foot stand, and an adult cat can jump much higher. Keep raising the stand until you find your cat's limit.

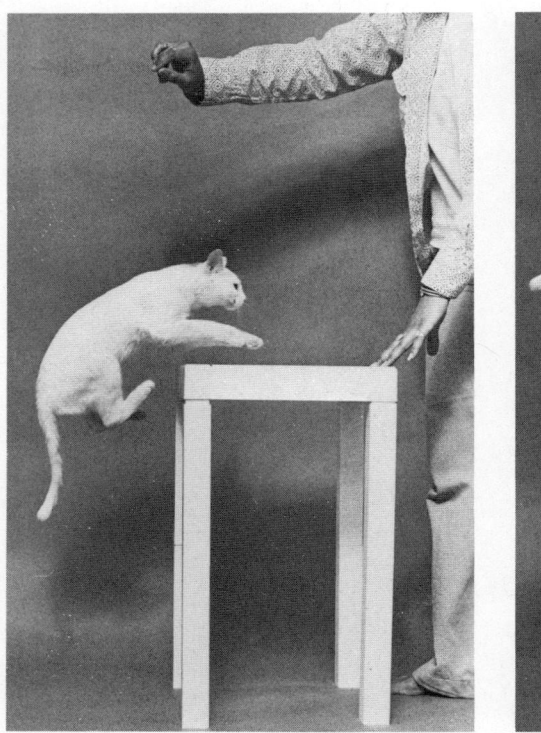

Kelly, the author's older cat, can jump a lot higher than little Aaron.

Jumping Off a Stand

Once your cat has learned the previous trick, this one should be easy. Start with the cat sitting on the stand. Then tell him to come, while slowly pushing him off the stand toward you. Repeat this lesson several times a day.

You may again find it easier to train your cat with the help of the leash. Put the leash on the cat and pull the cat toward you, off the stand, while ordering him to come. Once he starts responding to

After a little practice, Aaron doesn't need a leash anymore.

the order alone, without waiting for the tug of the leash, take the leash off and repeat the process.

You cat should learn this trick within two days, but don't be surprised if he learns it much faster. Many cats take only an hour or so to learn these tricks, once they have learned to come to you on command. Have your cat practice jumping on and off the stand several times a day until you are sure he understands what he's doing. With young cats especially, it's a good idea to have them practice everything, including leash walking and coming on command, because their attention spans are short and they are apt to forget things from one day to the next.

When your cat has mastered these basic tricks, you can advance to more complicated ones.

Jumping from One Stand to Another

Place two stands of equal height very close together. Command you cat to jump onto the first one. Then walk back, away from the second stand, and tell him to come to you. Make sure he walks over

"This doesn't look so tough. . . . Hey, wait a minute. She's moving these tables farther and farther apart."

Training 25

both stands to get to you. After he's done this a few times, you can begin to set the stands farther and farther apart. It will be hard for him to walk from one stand to the next, so he will have to jump. Again, it may be easier to start this training with the leash on, removing it as the cat becomes proficient.

Once the cat knows the basic procedure, you can move the stands as far apart as the cat can jump. Soon he will be performing spectacular long-distance leaps. Even a little kitten like Aaron can jump thirty-three inches—almost three feet!

"I think I'd rather fool around . . . but she won't let me . . . so I'll have to show her what I can do—thirty-three inches!"

26 *The Truth About Cats*

Training 27

Jumping Through Hoops

Hoops are used in many tricks, but start by teaching your cat to walk through a hoop on the ground. You can buy hoops in a toy store or in the toy section of a department store. The hoops I use are rings cut from plastic flowerpots, about nine or ten inches in diameter. The hoops you see in the pictures are attached to telescoping rods so that they can be raised or lowered, and turned from side to side. The hoops themselves are attached to the rods with masking tape. The rods are then attached to a wooden or plastic board.

Place the cat in a sitting position on the floor. Hold or place a

In the beginning, before Aaron understands what he's supposed to do, the author shows him by moving him along by hand.

hoop in front of him, right at floor level, and push him through it, while giving the command to come. When he has the hang of it, begin to raise the hoop a couple of inches at a time. If he has trouble, just keep guiding him through the hoop. You may want to put the leash on the cat and pull him gently through the hoop.

When he has learned to go through one hoop, start adding more. He will go through one, then another, and another.

The first day, Aaron suddenly figures it out, and off he goes through Hoop No. 1.

30 *The Truth About Cats*

A reflective moment, and then through the next one.

Training 31

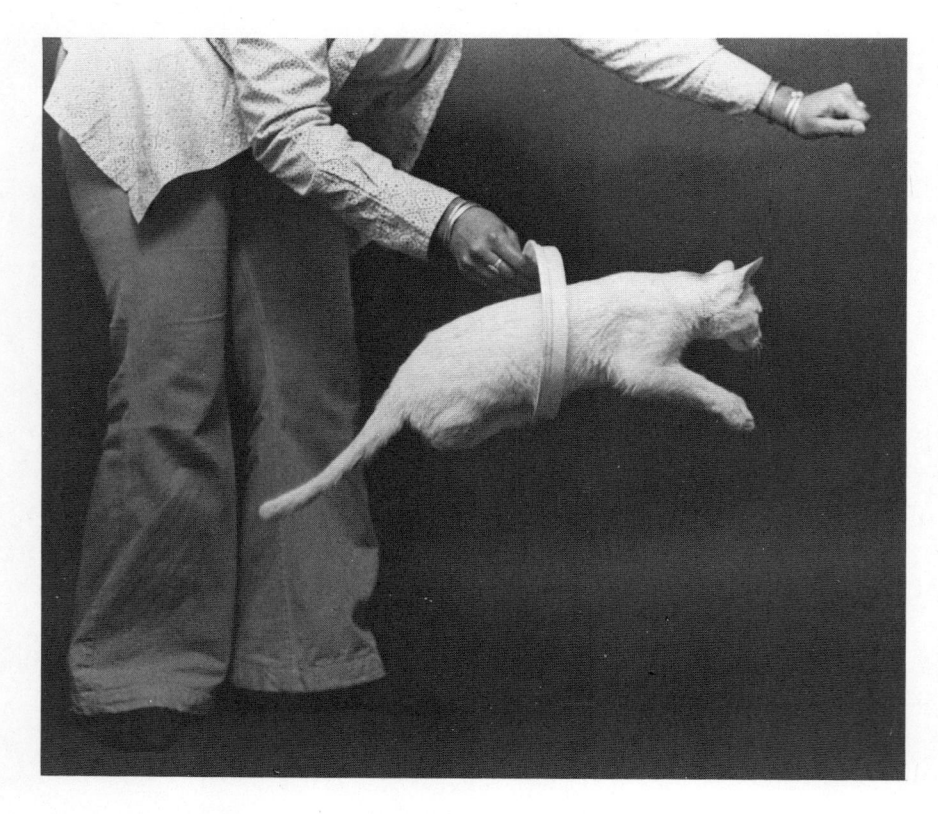

Kelly, a veteran at this sort of thing, shows the kid how to take a high one.

Jumping Through Hoops and Onto a Stand

When the cat knows the previous trick, you can add a stand. Set the stand about twenty inches from the last hoop. Place the cat in front of the hoop, go behind the stand, and tell him to come. He will go through the hoop and then jump onto the stand. He may need to practice jumping onto the stand before you try this. Again, the leash may help in the training.

Once your cat learns this trick, you can add more hoops for greater effect.

Jumping from One Stand, Through a Hoop, to Another Stand

If your cat can jump from stand to stand, and can also go through hoops, he shouldn't have much trouble learning this trick. Place two stands as far apart as your cat can jump (usually about three feet) and place a hoop between them. Command the cat to come. He will want to ignore the hoop completely, and jump around it to the other stand, so you will probably have to pick him up and push him through it a few times until he gets the idea. If he has trouble going through the hoop, try practicing for a while with the hoop near the floor. When you re-set it to the height of the stands, your cat should have no further problem. Using the leash may also help. Soon the cat will be jumping from one stand to the other, going through the hoop on the way.

"She doesn't really expect me to jump through *the hoop to get to the other table does she?"*

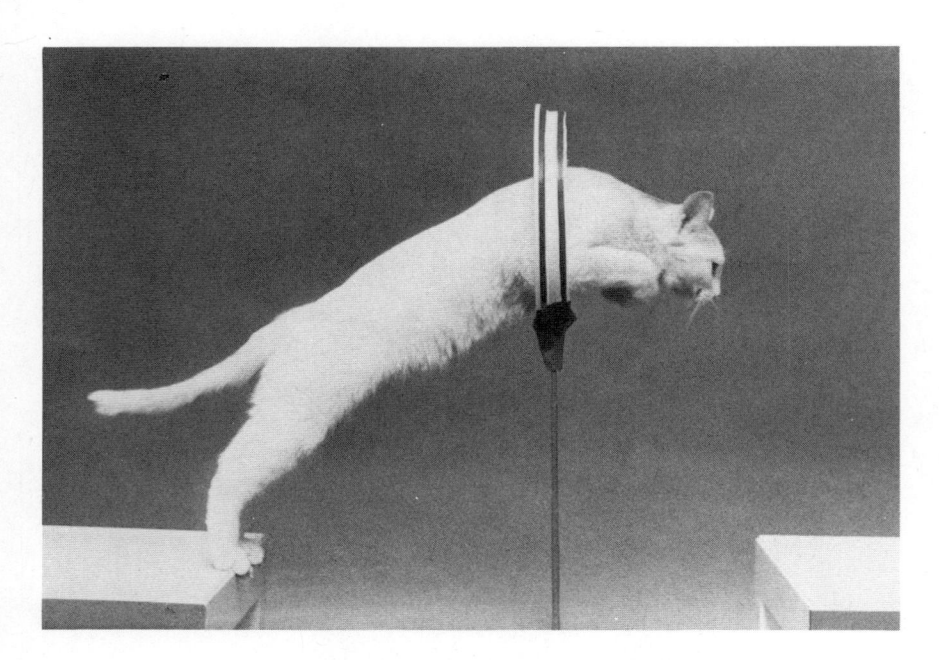

Kelly shows Aaron that table-hoop-table is no sweat. . . .

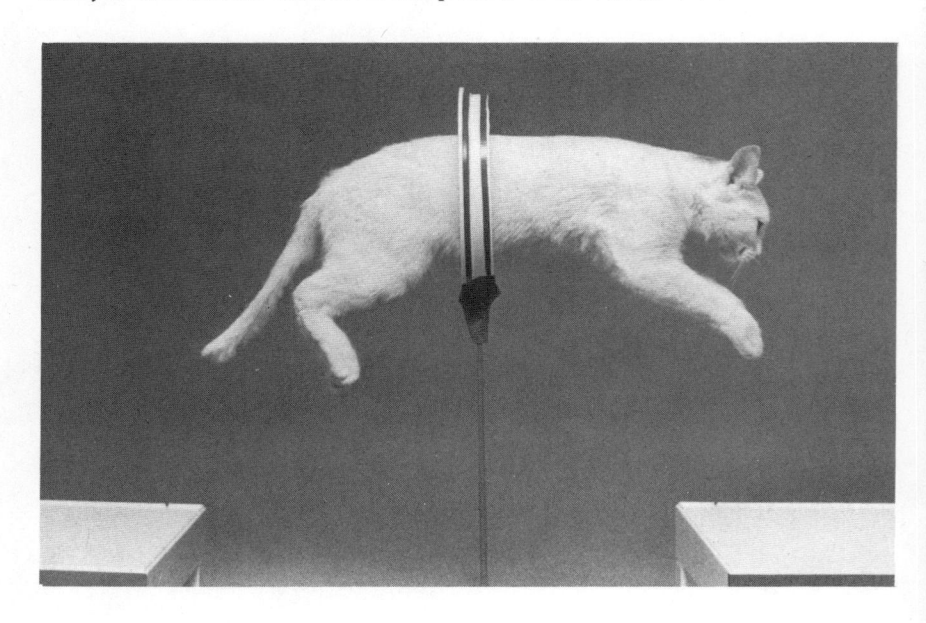

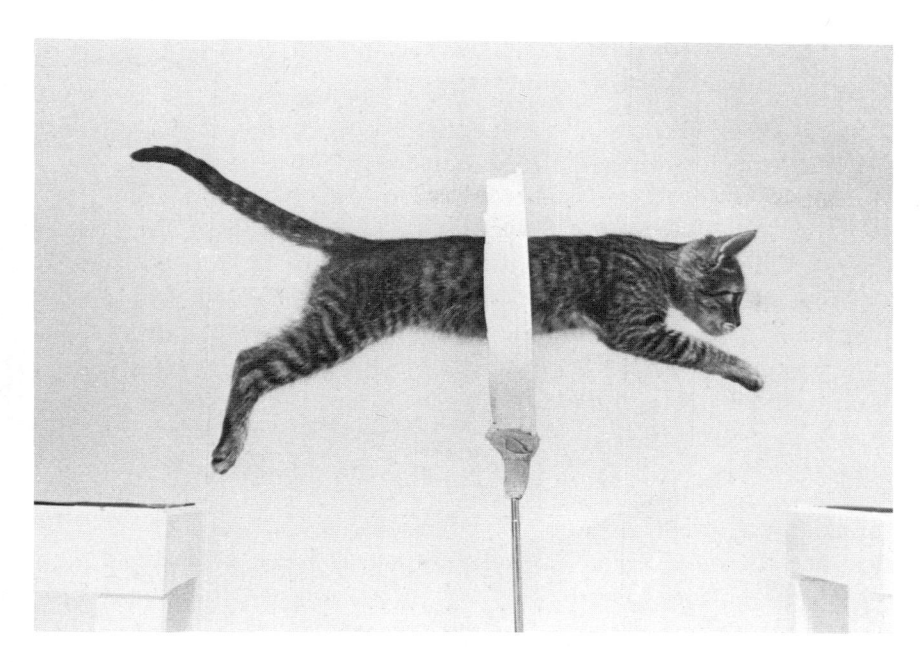

... *and our hero pulls it off beautifully.*

Jumping from One Stand to the Floor and Then to Another Stand

This is one of the easiest tricks to teach. Set up two stands, too far apart for the cat to leap from one to the other. Place the cat on one stand and command him to come. He may try to leap, but finding it too long a jump, he will jump to the floor, run, and jump up to the other stand. If he has trouble, try guiding him with the leash a few times. Some cats will be upset by the distance between the stands and will refuse to move at all. In this case, simply push the cat off the stand, to the ground, and then up onto the second stand. Do this a few times until he knows it on his own.

Going Through a Tunnel

Your cat can go through a tunnel as well as through a hoop. You can easily make a tunnel from heavy posterboard. I use a plastic flowerpot with the bottom cut out. Just put the tunnel in your cat's path and tell him to come. He will immediately go around it to get to you. Put him back, push him through the tunnel a few times, and he'll quickly catch on.

"After that other stuff, this tunnel seems awfully easy."

You can then combine the tunnel with the stand. He will jump off the stand and go through the tunnel, or go through the tunnel and jump onto the stand, or both.

Walking Up and Down Ladders

Cats will go up and down ladders. The ladders I use are actually trellises, which can be purchased in a plant store. Place a ladder on either side of your cat's stand. Be sure to tape them securely to the stand. If they slip and the cat falls, the accident will be a big blow to his confidence, and it may be many days before you can persuade him to try this trick again.

Now, place the cat at the foot of one of the ladders and order him to come. He may refuse to climb it at all, or he may jump off the ladder before reaching the stand, or he may try to jump onto the stand, bypassing the ladder completely. If so, just push him up it, across the stand, and down the other ladder. Or use the leash to guide him. You will know whether your cat learns faster with the

Aaron inches his way up the wobbly ladder.

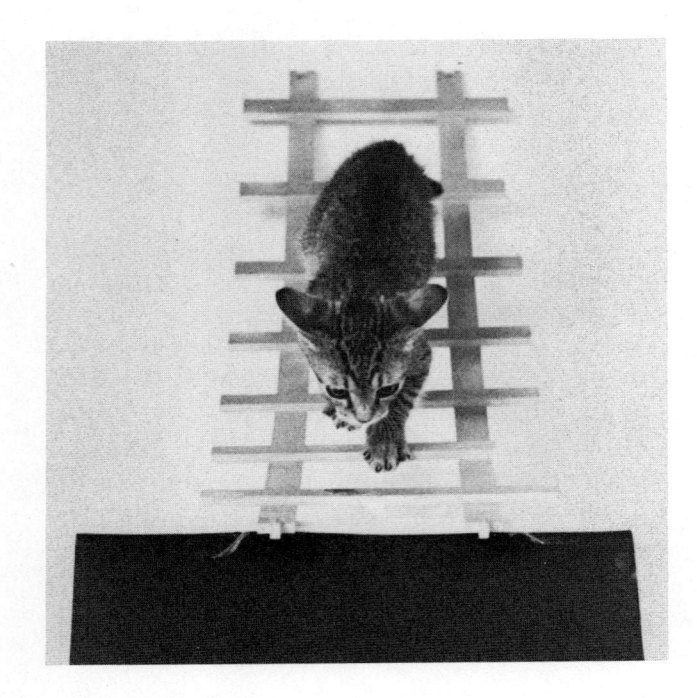

When he gets to the top, he'll have to go down on the other side.

leash or without it. After about five or six attempts, he should be able to do this trick without help. If not, keep trying until he learns it. He will.

Your cat can also climb a ladder as high as five feet. Start with a short one, increasing the length every day. You can push him or guide him with the leash at first.

Walking a Narrow Board

Start by using a wide board, then narrower and narrower ones during each practice session. Set up the board between two stands. Be sure it is securely anchored. Place the cat on one stand, get behind the other one, and tell him to come. You will have to push him across the board or use the leash as a guide the first few times. Within half an hour, though, he should be walking across the board very happily. Decrease the board's width each day until your cat is crossing a board only one and a half inches wide. If he can go over an even narrower one, fine.

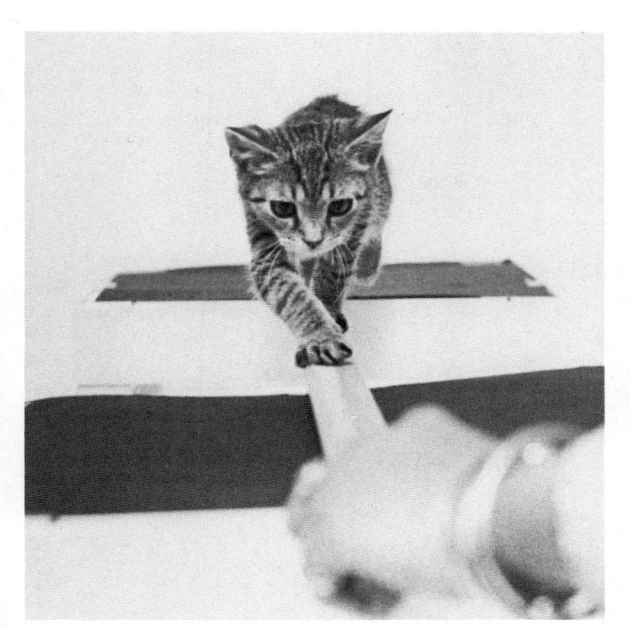

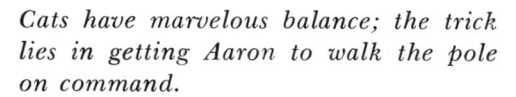

Cats have marvelous balance; the trick lies in getting Aaron to walk the pole on command.

Training 39

Jumping Hurdles

Believe it or not, this is not a hard trick for your cat to learn. You will need hurdles, which can be purchased in a sporting goods store. I make mine out of cardboard, bent in the center, as you see in the pictures.

Start by setting up a very low hurdle, about three or four inches high, depending on the size of your cat. Put the cat in front of it and order him to come. He will immediately try to go around it to get to you. Stop him and put him back in position. You will have to push him over the hurdle, or guide him over it with the leash a few times before he will jump it on command. If he refuses to jump the hurdle, try making it lower. The important thing, though, is to persevere. Once your cat learns this trick, you can begin to make the hurdles higher—up to whatever height your cat can jump.

You can also teach your cat to jump over more than one hurdle. Simply set up two hurdles at a time, using low ones at first. Put the hurdles too close together for the cat to jump between them and he'll have to go over both. Now add another, and another. Or set them too far apart for the cat to leap over all at once, and he'll go over one, then the next, then the next. Set up the hurdles in any combination you want. Whenever you have trouble getting the cat to jump, put on his leash and guide him that way.

And now, the High Hurdles. One small leap for a little cat, but a great leap for cat-kind.

Training 41

Once the cat knows these tricks, you can combine them in many different ways.

Most young cats will learn any of the foregoing tricks within an hour, but you may have to teach them in fifteen-minute sessions over a few days. If at any time you see your cat getting tired, or unhappy with the training, it may be best to let him rest and to work again later or the next day. But do not let your cat use sulky, fretful, stubborn behavior to get out of training altogether. If you think he's just acting up for no reason, make him work. You know your cat best and will have to judge when he's really tired and when he's being lazy. Remember, never let him get the upper hand. If you do, you will soon have an obstinate, spoiled cat on your hands.

4
Etiquette

This chapter covers a few aspects of good manners in cats. It is not comprehensive. If your cat has an irritating habit not discussed here, remember that obedience training does work. Be consistent—scold your cat *every time* he disobeys you. It may take time, but if you let him know you will not tolerate bad behavior, he will learn to shape up.

Affection

Most people want affectionate cats. You can encourage your cat to be more affectionate by paying a lot of attention to him. Pet him often. Whenever you see him, go up to him, talk to him softly, and stroke him. If you do this many times a day, you will have a loving, purring cat who enjoys your company. It is best to start affection training while the kitten is small, when he is naturally warm and affectionate. He will develop a great disposition and will not lose it when he grows up. Remember that if you are a distant and unfriendly owner, your cat will develop the same traits. If you want him to be close to you, you have to be close to him.

Housebreaking

Housebreaking a kitten is simple. Fill a pan with litter or clay. After the kitten has eaten, watch him carefully. He will soon look for a place to relieve himself and will meow and scratch the floor. Immediately put him into his pan and praise him after he uses it. He will quickly learn to prefer his pan to other places.

If, however, you have a kitten who consistently uses an area other than his pan, yell at him and lightly slap his hindquarters. The area he seems to prefer should be thoroughly cleaned with a strong cleanser, such as ammonia, which will kill the scent and prevent the kitten from returning to the same spot. If your kitten proves to be a slow learner, it may be best to keep him confined to one room until he understands what you expect from him.

Scratching

A cat who scratches furniture does so because he is trying to shorten his nails. In the wild, he would be walking on rocks and using his nails in ways that would naturally shorten them. In your home, however, the nails need regular trimming. If your cat's nails are short enough he won't have to scratch your furniture.

Start cutting a kitten's nails at an early age. In fact, the sooner the better. Using a nail clipper or nail scissors, cut them as short as possible without cutting the blood vessel. You can see this red vessel in the nail. If you should cut the vessel by accident, don't worry. A tissue applied to the nail will stop the bleeding within a few minutes. A kitten's nails must be cut every week. If you let them grow long, the kitten will develop the bad habit of scratching, which will be hard to break later on.

Some cats do, however, scratch furniture for fun or because they are bored. Whenever you see your kitten or cat doing this, yell "no" at him and slap him lightly across the hindquarters. You must do this *every time* he scratches. Let him know you are in charge, and he will soon stop.

I do not believe in buying a scratching post for a cat. It only encourages a cat to scratch, even when his nails do not need to be shortened. Soon he will get bored with the post and start using the furniture. It is best to avoid this problem altogether by keeping his nails short and teaching him, firmly, to keep his claws off the furniture.

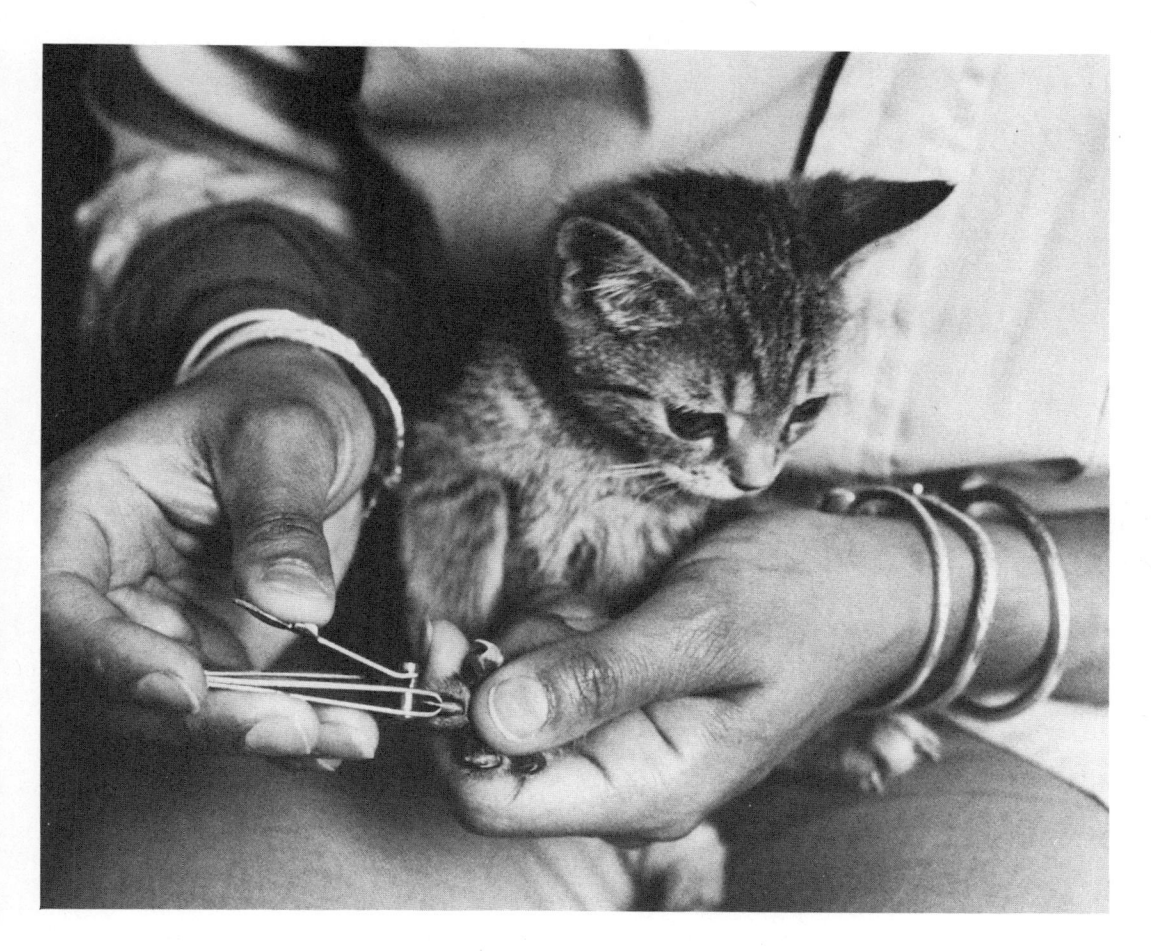

Weekly nail clippings help keep cats from scratching the furniture.

House Plants

Many cats eat house plants. The main reason for this is that they are not regularly given vegetables in their diets. A cat eats plants because he is longing for vegetation. It is not true that cats who eat vegetables assume plants are the same and eat them too. Feeding your cat a well-balanced diet will control this bad behavior (see Chapter Six).

I have lots of plants, many of which are on low stands close to the ground. My cats could easily reach them and eat them if they wanted to, but they don't. They seem to have a sixth sense about them—they "know" the plants mean a lot to me.

You too can train your cat to keep away from your plants. Whenever you see him go near the plants, yell "stop" or "no," and slap him lightly on the hindquarters. If you start training a kitten this way, he will learn very fast. An older cat will learn more slowly, but he *will* learn, *if* you are consistent and tenacious. Cats should learn that plants are only to look at, not to eat. If your cat respects you, he will sense that the plants are important to you, which will help you keep him away from them.

A combination of diet and discipline will end the house-plant-eating problem.

The Noisy Cat

Many cats meow loudly and walk under your feet while you are preparing their meals. The cat doesn't seem to understand that you know he's hungry. He thinks he has to make noise or you will forget to feed him. He will usually meow nonstop until his food is placed in front of him.

You can easily stop this annoying habit. Use a food mat. Set it on the floor in the cat's usual eating spot during the regular feeding time, but do not put food on it. Place the cat on the mat in a sitting position, leave him there, and begin fixing his meal. He will immediately get up, meowing after you. As soon as he leaves the mat, rush up to him, say "no," snap your fingers, slap him lightly on the hindquarters, and return him to the mat. Pet him, letting him know he's a good cat when he's on the mat. When he leaves the mat again, repeat the procedure—over and over if necessary. You will probably have to do this a great many times before he learns. Not until he is sitting quietly on the mat should you bring him his food. Eventually, he will realize that he will not be served until he is quiet. Your cat should learn this within one day.

Grooming and Exercise

Grooming a cat is essentially quite simple, and I will therefore discuss just a couple of points I feel are important. Exercise, however, is another problem. Most cats do not get enough exercise. They grow fat and lazy. If they learn to do tricks, of course, that is wonderful exercise, but you can also follow the suggestions below.

The Cat's Coat

Shedding can be an annoying problem. Most kittens shed their baby hair at about three months of age. At five months their permanent hair has usually come in. Adult cats shed a lot of hair during the summer and when they are handled or played with. Except for this normal shedding, you should not have any trouble with your cat's fur if you feed him a healthful diet and brush him regularly.

The quality of a cat's hair depends a great deal on the quality of his food. Commercial boxed or canned food will produce dull, lifeless hair, but a cat fed natural foods will develop a healthy, glossy coat that sheds very little. Your cat's diet should include vegetables, fruits, nuts, brewer's yeast, soybean meal, and wheat germ (see Chapter Six). If your cat's fur is unhealthy, try mixing peanut oil or whole

A performer owes it to his audience to stay well-groomed.

peanuts into his food. His coat should improve noticeably within a month or so.

The Cat's Whiskers

There are many misconceptions about a cat's whiskers. Some so-called authorities claim that if a cat loses his whiskers, he loses all of his sense of touch and will panic and refuse to go through small openings. This is not true. Whiskers may be used for some sense of touch but they are not the only things the cat relies on. If a cat knows his surroundings, temporary loss of his whiskers—which will grow back—will not disturb him.

Sometimes a cat's whiskers will break from brushing against the sides of small or narrow hoops. This is not a problem. A broken whisker will always grow back within a few weeks, and no psychological problems will develop for the cat. My cat Kelly has often lost all his whiskers in one day when I was using extra small hoops to create a dramatic effect. It has never bothered him at all. The same thing has happened to Aaron and to a few other kittens with no harmful results. In my observation, a cat's whiskers are like a woman's long fingernails—they may be nice to look at but they serve no useful purpose. If they did, would Kelly and Aaron continue to perform the tricks in this book? Certainly not.

The Cat's Ears

A cat's ears should be cleaned once a week to remove dirt and wax and to prevent ear mites. First wash the ears with warm water. Then, using a cotton swab dipped in rubbing alcohol or mineral oil, clean inside the ears. Be very gentle and clean only the area you can see. Probing too deep into the ear could cause serious damage. After cleaning, be sure to dry the ears thoroughly.

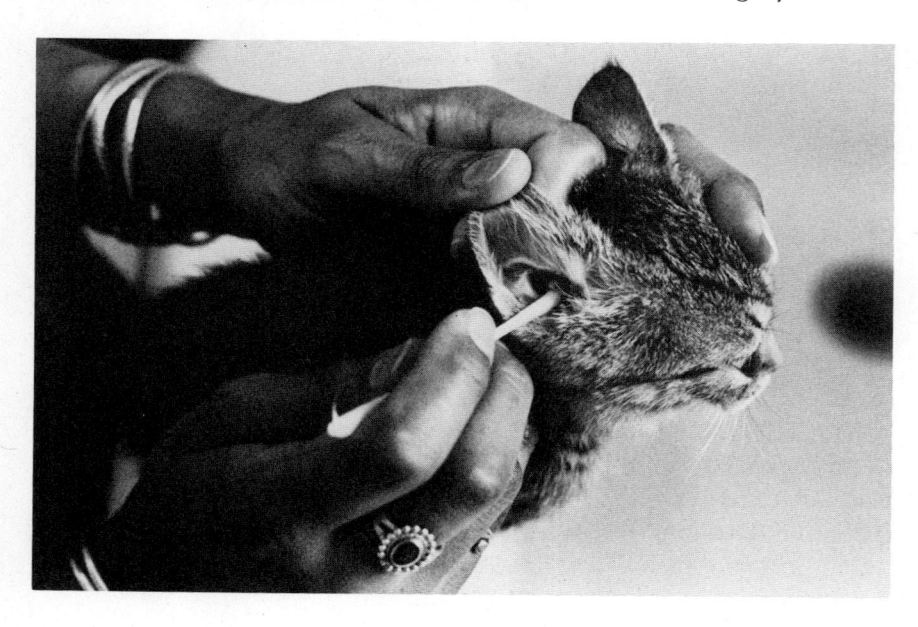

If your cat is constantly scratching his head, neck, or ears, he may have ear mites. You cannot always see them. If the scratching persists even after a thorough cleaning, take the cat to a veterinarian.

Bathing

Cats should be bathed regularly, once a week. You can start this when they get to be about two months old. I put my cats in the bathtub and use a hand shower. During the shower, you can clean the ears and brush the teeth to remove tartar. Bathing will also remove loose hairs that could cause a shedding problem. After the shower, dry the cat thoroughly and brush him with a good-quality brush.

If you start bathing your cat at an early age, you will usually have no trouble. Most cats will learn to like the water. An adult

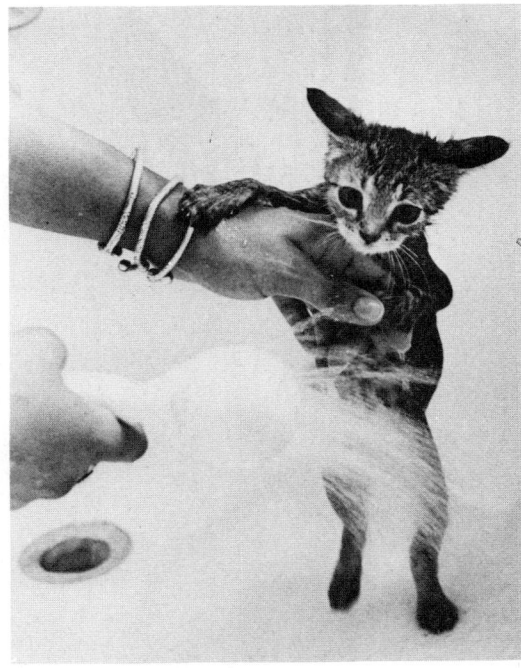

Aaron's first bath with soap and water—not so bad.

Grooming and Exercise 51

cat who has never been bathed may, however, resist violently. Put the cat into the tub and give him a very short shower, using warm water. Keep him in for just a couple of minutes. If he starts to panic, reassure him with lots of petting. If he is still frantic, tell him firmly to stop. Let him know you will not give in to him. It may take three or four baths before he adjusts to the water, but if you are persistent he will settle down. He will probably even learn to like it, which will be nice because you can then teach him to swim, a wonderful exercise for a cat.

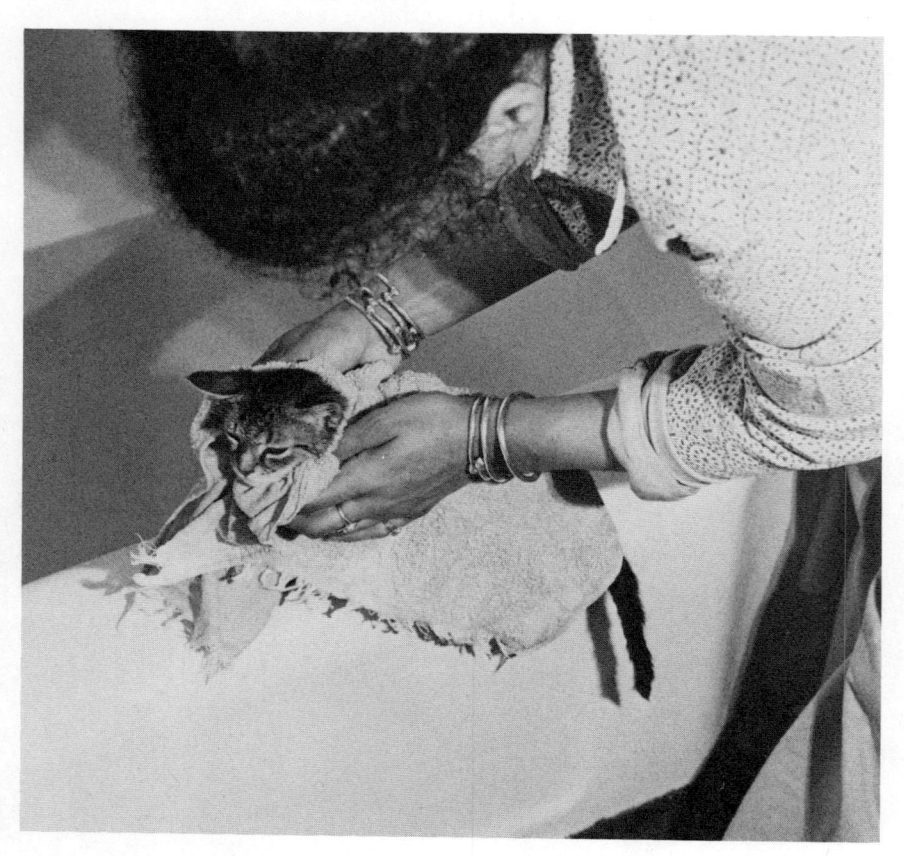

After his bath, Aaron gets a thorough drying. He likes to snuggle up in the towel.

Exercise: Walking and Swimming

Cats need exercise, just like people, if they are going to be healthy and good-looking. Lack of exercise encourages laziness, and many lazy cats tend to be spoiled and bad-tempered.

Walking is one good exercise. When your cat is leash-trained (see Chapter Three), you should walk him for half an hour every day. It is best to walk him outdoors, so he can get some fresh air and sunshine, but if the weather is bad walk him inside instead.

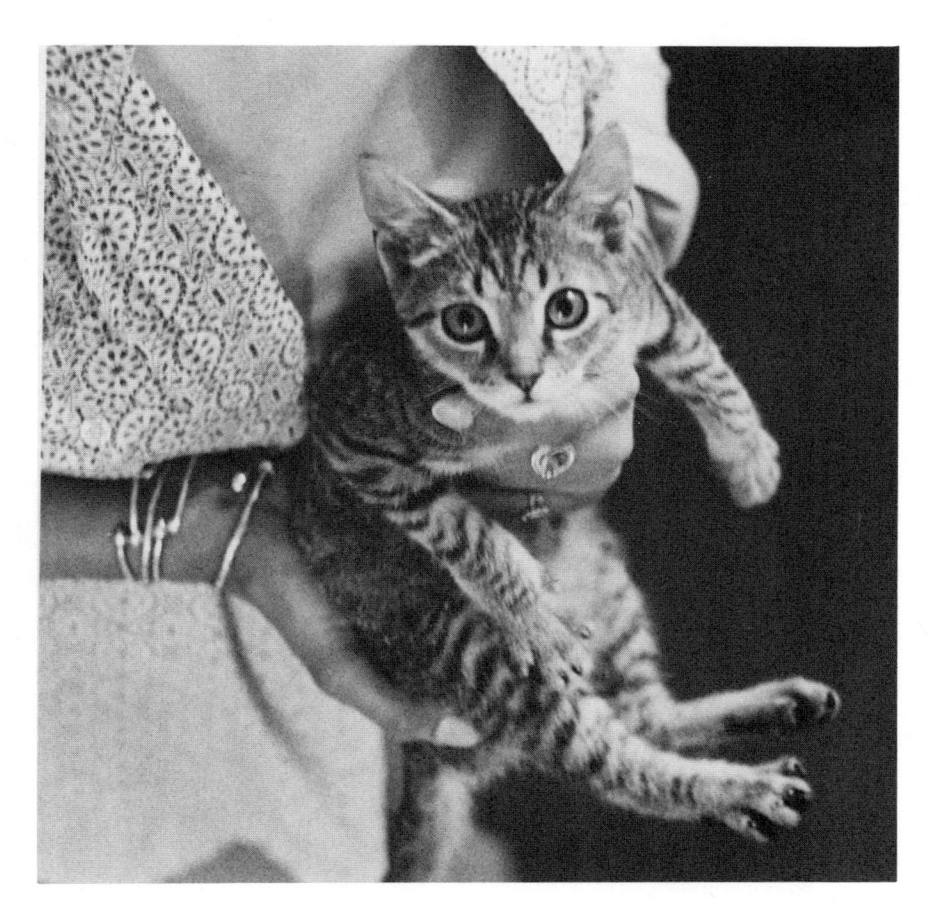

Here he is, all bathed and brushed and ready for anything.

Sometimes, after his bath, Aaron likes to take a few turns around the tub. Swimming is fabulous exercise and keeps him slim and fit.

54 *The Truth About Cats*

Swimming is also terrific for cats. Once your cat has stopped complaining and has gotten used to water, try filling the tub with warm water at the end of his bath. Let him swim for five minutes or so. Swimming is a natural movement for him—you don't have to teach him how to do it. Later, increase his swimming time to fifteen minutes. You can let your cat swim in the bathtub for fifteen minutes at a time, once or twice a week. Don't use soap on him during these exercise periods, towel him dry thoroughly after his swim, and keep him warm and out of drafts. This exercise strengthens your cat's legs and tightens his muscles. Cats who swim have strong healthy bodies that are lean and muscular with no sign of fat.

Between laps, Aaron takes a tubside breather.

Grooming and Exercise

The Water Baby.

6
Diet

All my cats are vegetarians. In my opinion, a meat diet makes a cat ill-tempered and uncooperative. Meat-eating cats tend to have bad dispositions. They also tend to become very finicky and demanding about their food. A well-balanced vegetarian diet, however, makes a cat healthy and happy and gives him a lovely sleek coat and pleasant breath.

A vegetarian diet that gives a cat all the protein, vitamins, and minerals he needs is certainly preferable to the usual diet of commercial cat food, which often consists of animal by-products and may have a certain amount of ash. You may think that a natural diet should include fresh meat and fish, since that is what a cat in the wild would eat. It's true that cats in the wild are meat eaters, but I have found that vegetarian cats are happier, calmer, and more affectionate than cats who eat meat.

Although I have never switched an older cat from a meat diet to a vegetarian one, I think it could be easily done. You might start by mixing vegetables, nuts, wheat germ, etc. in with your cat's regular meals. Once he's gotten used to the taste of the new food, start using more vegetables and less meat. Find out what his favorite vegetable is and add it to every meal. Then gradually decrease the amount of

Aaron doesn't know that felines are supposed to be carnivores. He eats his vegetarian platter eagerly.

meat in each meal until he is eating no meat at all. You will now have a completely vegetarian cat.

Protein, Vitamins, and Minerals

Cats need protein in their diets, but it need not come from meat. Cheese, milk, brewer's yeast, and soybean meal are all high in protein. The sample menus in this chapter contain more than enough protein from such nonmeat sources. The vitamins and minerals cats need are also available from foods other than meat. The meals I outline below contain all a cat needs of these nutrients.

Vitamin C

I want to add a special note about vitamin C. When my cat Kelly was sick with a stomach virus, the veterinarian told me his condition was hopeless and that he would certainly die. He seemed to be in a coma, awake for only minutes at a time. I decided to try force-feeding him vitamin C, in the form of pineapple juice. Using an eyedropper, I fed him a mixture of ninety percent juice and ten percent evaporated milk. An hour later, Kelly was wide awake and healthy. It was a miraculous recovery. I include this story to suggest that, if you have a sick cat, try giving him vitamin C. You have nothing to lose and everything to gain. You should always, of course, make sure your cat has plenty of vitamin C in his regular diet.

Meals

The daily meals I feed my cats consist mainly of mixed vegetables, potatoes, fruits, nuts, rice, soybean meal, whole-wheat bread, wheat germ, wheat-germ oil, peanut oil, and brewer's yeast, with milk or water. I prefer fresh or frozen vegetables, boiled until soft, to the canned variety. Occasionally I give my cats meat-flavored foods such as chicken broth, but I find that they soon grow tired of this and want to get back to their vegetables.

Kittens six weeks to five months old need to be fed four times a day. After five months, you can start feeding them twice a day, or even once, depending on your schedule. Feed a small kitten soft food, mixed with milk. When the cat is older, he can chew hard food.

You will notice that your cat will soon show a preference for certain foods. Never serve him his favorite food alone. Instead, mix it with other food to make sure he eats a balanced meal. Jason, for instance, loves green peas, so I mix them with whole-wheat bread and rice. Serve many different combinations of foods so your cat won't get bored eating the same thing day after day. Alternate the vegetable and fruit dishes. And if your cat drinks water have a bowl of it available for him.

Menus

Below are examples of typical meals. Serve any of these dishes to your cat at each feeding. Mix and match the various ingredients to create your own meals.

1. Tender cooked white or brown rice, mixed with chopped, lightly cooked onions, potatoes, and spinach. You can add salt.
2. Lightly toasted whole-wheat bread, fortified with toasted or raw wheat germ, soybean meal, and wheat-germ oil. Serve at room temperature, either chunky or finely crushed, according to your cat's preference.
3. A combination of Swiss, American, and cottage cheese, mixed with whole or evaporated milk and heavy cream. Any combination of hard and soft cheeses could be used.
4. Cooked green beans, peas, lima beans, and rice, mixed with brewer's yeast and a small amount of peanut oil.
5. Lightly cooked chopped onions, mixed with green peas.
6. Lightly cooked mixed vegetables, including onions, combined with raw soybean meal and peanut oil. You can add crushed peanuts to this.
7. Lightly cooked green peas, mixed with brewer's yeast and peanuts.
8. Buttered rice mixed with lightly cooked onions.
9. Cooked rice and soft American (or other) cheese, mixed with crumbled whole-wheat bread.
10. Potatoes, onions, and mixed vegetables cooked together for ten minutes.
11. Cooked mixed vegetables with wheat germ and wheat-germ oil.
12. A combination of raw raisins, oranges, and bananas.
13. Shredded wheat, slightly softened in milk, mixed with wheat germ, toasted whole-wheat bread, and wheat-germ oil.

14. Cooked rice mixed with raisins, fresh banana, pear, lettuce, celery, soybean meal, and peanut oil. You can add butter.
15. Lightly cooked mixed vegetables, mixed with pear and raisins.
16. Raw celery with cherries, orange, and raisins.
17. American or other cheese, mixed with banana and peanut oil.

7

General Care

This chapter deals with some of the common health problems that affect cats. It is not meant to be a complete guide to your cat's health care, just selected observations and advice. I recommend that a cat be taken to the veterinarian for regular checkups. He should also, of course, see a vet when he is obviously ill and does not respond to treatment.

Unweaned Kittens

A kitten is normally weaned at the age of five or six weeks. This means he is no longer nursing and can eat solid food. If you find or buy a kitten younger than this, he will require a great deal of special care.

The unweaned kitten should be fed finely ground baby food and evaporated milk. If he won't eat, put some food on his mouth so he will have to lick it up, or use an eyedropper to feed him. You will have to feed him like this at least four times a day until he learns to eat by himself. An hour after each meal, bathe his genital area with warm water to stimulate evacuation. The very young kitten cannot eliminate body wastes without help. When he is about five weeks old, start feeding the kitten soft foods, slowly easing him into a regular diet (see Chapter Six).

A kitten this young demands a lot of time and work from you, but remember that all the attention you give him will draw him very close to you. The kitten will grow up thinking of you as his mother. The six unweaned kittens I have cared for in the past were all more affectionate and more attached to me than the older kittens I have bought in pet stores.

Shots

A new kitten should be given a number of shots to protect against rabies, pneumonia, feline panleukopenia, feline distemper, and virus diseases. The ASPCA or any veterinarian can administer these shots. A kitten should be six to eight weeks old when he gets them. Consult with the vet about when later shots should be given.

Teething

Opinions vary on this subject. Some vets say kittens do teethe; others insist they do not. I believe they do. How else can I explain the constant chewing so many kittens do during the time their baby teeth are coming out?

Kittens may teethe from the age of six weeks to four months. Some show no sign of pain. Others will chew on clothing, pencils, or almost anything else. If your kitten does this, give him something safe and sanitary to chew on. I have found that when a kitten starts to chew, he will have a better appetite. It is best not to try to prevent this normal behavior.

Altering

Unless your cat is going to be bred, it's best to have him or her altered. This will prevent a male from spraying urine in the house and will keep a female from producing an unwanted litter.

A male should be castrated at between six and nine months of age. This is a simple operation, which is done by a veterinarian. The cat should be back home the next day. A female should be spayed when she is about eight months old. This operation may keep her at the vet's for two days.

There is no change of temperament or personality in an altered cat. A male will not gain weight, either, if the operation is done at an early age (six to nine months). You can also feed the cat less if his previous diet is now too much for him, and you can give him regular exercise. The only personality difference between an intact and an altered cat is that the latter is no longer interested in sex.

Colds and Viruses

Cats can catch colds or virus infections. When a cat has a cold, he has a runny nose, a high fever, and difficulty in breathing. He may also sneeze, lose his appetite, become listless, and sleep a great deal. Excessive thirst and urination are also symptoms.

You should keep the cat warm and out of drafts. Feed him lots of fruit and fruit juices mixed with his regular food. If his condition doesn't clear up in about a week, take him to the vet.

Eyes

Squinting, tearing, or a white discharge at the corners of the eye is usually a sign of a cold or virus and will clear up when the cold does. Persistent eye trouble may indicate an allergy or possibly distemper. The cat should be taken to the vet for diagnosis and treatment.

Tongue

Cuts or ulcerations on the tongue are also symptoms of a cold or virus. They may prevent the cat from eating, so if your cat loses his appetite you might check his tongue. Treat him as you would for a cold. If the symptoms persist, however, the cat should see a vet.

Diarrhea

Colds or virus infections can cause diarrhea. Use the same remedy as for colds. Another cause could be allergy, which would have to be diagnosed by a doctor. Diarrhea can also result from overfeeding.

You can treat your cat by giving him Kaopectate. If the condition doesn't clear up in a week, take him to the vet.

Constipation

Constipation can be caused by a cold or a poor diet. Try treating the cat by giving him lots of liquids, vegetables, and plenty of exercise. Walk him outdoors for an hour. Give him milk of magnesia or petroleum jelly by putting it on his paw or mouth so that he will lick it off. If the condition persists for more than a week, see the vet to be sure there's not a serious problem.

Vomiting

Vomiting has many possible causes. It may be the result of a cold or virus (see treatment for colds, above). It may be a temporary reaction to overeating, hairballs, or an injection. It may be caused by parasites or allergies that have to be diagnosed and treated by a vet. It may indicate nervousness. Try giving the cat Kaopectate. If symptoms persist longer than a week, consult the vet.

Worms

The common signs of worms are vomiting, diarrhea or constipation, nervousness, loss of appetite and of weight, and a rough coat. You can not always see worms in the cat's feces. If you suspect worms, take the cat to the vet.

Scratching

A cat will scratch himself excessively because of skin disease, parasites, or allergy. Examine him thoroughly for red skin, scales, bumps, or fleas. If he has fleas, use one of the commercially available flea remedies. If he shows signs of skin disease, he should see the vet. Remember, too, that your cat may scratch just out of nervousness. If so, try to find another outlet for his energy.

Panting

Many cats will naturally pant after exercise and during the summer. If your cat pants excessively in the summer, try to keep him cool. Avoid overheating him with too much exercise. Wet his paws and tail with cool water.

Bad Breath

While a cat's baby teeth are falling out and his adult teeth are coming in, he may develop bad breath. The problem will end after this—unless he eats too much meat. A meat-eating cat will often have unpleasant breath and a lot of tartar on his teeth. Feed your cat a well-balanced vegetarian diet, including hard foods like crisp toast or shredded wheat to remove tartar, and bad breath will not be a problem.

Deafness

Some cats are born deaf—especially white cats with blue eyes. This defect does not affect their behavior in any noticeable way, and such cats are just as easy to train as are cats with normal hearing.

Eyedroppers

There may be times when you have to force-feed a sick cat or a very young kitten, who could starve to death if he won't eat by himself. It is easiest to do so using an eyedropper filled with thoroughly ground baby food mixed with evaporated milk.

An eyedropper is an important health aid and should always be available.

Conclusion

Some people say that it is a shame to teach cats to do tricks. They are afraid that training will break a cat's spirit. This fear is unfounded. A trained cat is every bit as strong and independent as a cat that has led the usual house-cat life.

Most people know that dogs can be trained. I have owned dogs in the past and have found that many of them were not as quick to learn as my cats. It is true that dogs want to please their owners, but so do cats. Once your cat trusts and respects you, you will be amazed at how fast he can learn.

Of course, cats will have off-days when they would rather do nothing at all, but this is a common problem faced by trainers of all types of animals. And even on their off-days my cats strive to please me—they simply show less enthusiasm. During training sessions with many different kittens and cats, including my older cat Kelly, they have all showed that they enjoy pleasing me by purring loudly and continuously and by pushing and pulling (kneading) with their paws. Are these the actions of cats that hate losing their "independence?" Obviously not. After working with fifteen different cats I know that cats enjoy their trick-training program. Yours will too.

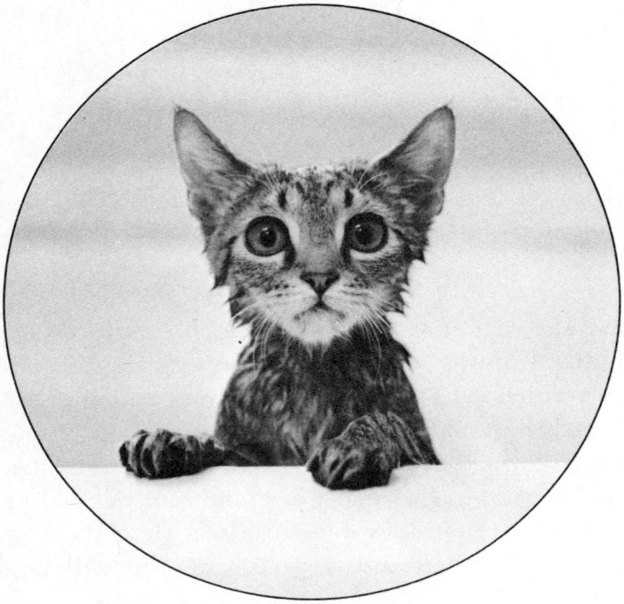